Saint John Paul II

Saint John Paul II

Be Not Afraid

Written by Susan Helen Wallace, FSP

Illustrated by Charlie Craig

Pauline
BOOKS & MEDIA
Boston

LoC data: The Library of Congress has cataloged an earlier edition of this book. LCCN: 2011004049

Published by Pauline Books & Media, 50 Saint Pauls Avenue, Boston, MA 02130-3491

Printed in the U.S.A.

SJPII KSEUSAHUDNHA8-221077 1178-6

www.pauline.org

Pauline Books & Media is the publishing house of the Daughters of St. Paul, an international congregation of women religious serving the Church with the communications media.

5 6 7 8 9 10   21 20 19 18 17

Encounter the Saints Series

Encounter the Saints Series

Blesseds Jacinta and Francisco Marto
Shepherds of Fatima

Blessed James Alberione
Media Apostle

Blessed Pier Giorgio Frassati
Journey to the Summit

Journeys with Mary
Apparitions of Our Lady

Saint Anthony of Padua
Fire and Light

Saint Andre Bessette
Miracles in Montreal

Saint Bernadette Soubirous
And Our Lady of Lourdes

Saint Catherine Labouré
And Our Lady of the Miraculous Medal

Saint Clare of Assisi
A Light for the World

Saint Elizabeth Ann Seton
Daughter of America

Saint Faustina Kowalska
Messenger of Mercy

Saint Francis of Assisi
Gentle Revolutionary

Saint Gianna Beretta Molla
The Gift of Life

Saint Ignatius of Loyola
For the Greater Glory of God

Saint Joan of Arc
God's Soldier

Saint John Paul II
Be Not Afraid

Saint Kateri Tekakwitha
Courageous Faith

Saint Martin de Porres
Humble Healer

Saint Maximilian Kolbe
Mary's Knight

Saint Pio of Pietrelcina
Rich in Love

Saint Teresa of Avila
Joyful in the Lord

Saint Thérèse of Lisieux
The Way of Love

Saint Thomas Aquinas
Missionary of Truth

Saint Thomas More
Courage, Conscience, and the King

For even more titles in the
Encounter the Saints series,
visit: www.pauline.org./EncountertheSaints

Contents

1

LOLEK

It had been a long winter in Wadowice (*Vad-o-VEE-chay*). Spring had been slow in coming, but now, as summer began, the trees were thick with green leaves. The warm weather brought new hope to the citizens of the little Polish town, located thirty miles southwest of Warsaw. Drawing aside a lace curtain, Mrs. Wojtyla (*Voy-TEE-wah*) smiled as she glanced out the window. *Summer is such a beautiful time of year,* she thought, *especially now that the war is over.* Her gaze returned to the cradle she was rocking. *And most especially since God has sent us little Karol!*

World War I, which raged from 1914 to 1918, had ended two years earlier. After 123 years of foreign occupation, Poland had finally regained its independence. Europe was at peace, at least for the moment. The young Wojtyla family—Emilia, her husband, Karol, and their son Edmund—were overjoyed at the birth of the newest family member on May 18, 1920. The infant boy was named Karol—the Polish equivalent of Charles—after his father.

It wasn't long though, before the chubby, rosy-cheeked baby was being called by the affectionate nickname Lolek (*LOW-leck*). (In English, Lolek would be similar to Charlie or Chuck.)

Emilia Wojtyla was a gentle, frail woman. Karol Wojtyla, Lolek's father, was a retired army officer. The couple were devoted to each other and to their children. Edmund was fourteen years older than Lolek. To his family and close friends, he was known as Mundek (*MOON-dek*), something like the nickname Eddie. Between the two boys, a girl had been born to Mr. and Mrs. Wojtyla. But she had lived only a short while.

Today, June 20, was special. Emilia carefully dressed her new baby in his long white baptismal robe. It was handmade of white linen and ruffles. Lolek looked perfect!

"He's ready to go, Papa," announced Emilia with a radiant smile. She wrapped her precious bundle in a light blanket to make sure he'd be warm enough. Mr. Wojtyla carried his infant son across the street to their parish, the Church of the Presentation of the Blessed Virgin Mary. There, Father Franciszek Zak, a military chaplain, baptized the little boy. Carefully pouring water over the baby's head, he pronounced the familiar words, "I baptize you, Karol Jozef Wojtyla, in the name of the Father, and of the Son, and of the Holy Spirit. Amen." Little Karol Jozef was now a member of the family of God.

Emilia and her husband sat on the couch that evening watching their new baby sleeping in his cradle. The couple said little to each other as they enjoyed the peace of the moment. Mundek curled up beside them with an interesting book. Emilia's imagination was hard at work. *What mother doesn't think her son or daughter is destined for greatness?* she asked herself. *What will Lolek become? We're simple, hard-working people. But my husband has so many good qualities—diligence, honesty, and prayerfulness, to name a few. And Mundek is such a wonderful boy. Karol Jozef will learn much from the good example of his father and brother. Of course, I want to help by being a loving mother. I can see it all now,* she smiled. *As soon as it gets warmer, I'll push my Lolek up and down the streets in his stroller. And I'll tell the neighbors who stop to admire him, "My Lolek is going to be a great man some day. Just wait and see! Yes, just wait and see!"*

2

LIFE WITH THE CAPTAIN

The Wojtylas lived in a comfortable second-floor apartment overlooking a courtyard. Mrs. Wojtyla often sat on the balcony and watched as Lolek and the other children played their games below. Lolek had many friends, but one of his closest was a Jewish boy named Jerzy Kluger. As they grew older, Lolek and Jerzy became experts at soccer, hiking, and swimming. In the winter, they played ice hockey on the frozen lakes and ponds.

September 15, 1926, marked a special date for Lolek. It was the day the six-year-old entered first grade. The school was just minutes away from his home. Lolek felt excited and very grown up. In the class of about sixty children, he anxiously searched for someone he knew. His face broke into a smile when he made a happy discovery. "Jerzy," he exclaimed in delight, "am I glad to see you!"

As the weeks flew by, Lolek and his classmates learned many new things. They studied history, religion, arithmetic, and the Polish language. They enjoyed singing, drawing, arts and crafts, and games. Lolek was always at the top of his class. He loved school.

But the young boy's peaceful life was soon to be shattered. When Lolek was in the third grade, his mother passed away. Forty-five-year-old Emilia had never been very healthy. She suffered from heart disease and other problems. Mrs. Wojtyla died on April 13, 1929, of kidney failure.

Lolek felt lonely and confused. His father, a sensitive, compassionate man, tried to bear up under his own grief. He had to be strong for his two boys, who deeply felt the loss of their mother. "Your Mama is in heaven with Jesus and Mary," Mr. Wojtyla comforted them. "She's no longer suffering."

"Can she still love us?" eight-year-old Lolek asked in a quivering voice.

"Yes, Lolek. Oh, yes," answered his father, pressing his youngest son to his chest. "Your Mama loves us more than ever now. She is very happy, and she's watching over us. Jesus has promised us that we will all be together again someday. Although we can't understand the reasons right now, we accept this sorrow from God's hands. We know that he allows everything for our good."

Lolek felt better just being with his father and hearing again about this promise of Jesus.

By this time, Mundek was living and studying at the university medical school. He came home as often as possible to spend time with his father and younger brother. Lolek loved his big brother. They would romp through the apartment, having a wonderful time. Lolek's dream was to have Mundek stay at home with him and his father. But for now that wasn't possible.

Mr. Wojtyla, often called "the Captain" by his neighbors because he had been in the army nearly thirty years, knew it was his responsibility to be both father and mother to Lolek. Now that his wife was gone, Mr. Wojtyla and his younger son faced big changes in their daily lives. The Captain was a quiet man, but he believed in keeping the lines of communication open between his children and himself. He also knew how to be organized without being rigid. He soon realized that he and Lolek had to develop a daily routine, and he wanted it to be workable for both of them.

I'm not a cook, the Captain admitted to himself. *Cooking was one of Emilia's gifts, and I'm sure she'd want me to do what's best for*

Lolek. The solution that he finally came up with was to have the family's midday meal together at a nearby restaurant. Mr. Wojtyla and Lolek said morning prayers and shared breakfast before Lolek left for school. Lolek returned home in the early afternoon, and he and his father walked the short distance to the restaurant.

Coming home after school later, Lolek always looked forward to playtime. That meant games, sports, and fun with his neighborhood friends for the next few hours. Then it was time for homework.

On rainy or snowy days, Mr. Wojtyla would teach an exciting history class from his well-read collection of books. Lolek was impressed with the way his papa could speak about Polish history and culture. The Captain loved his country and was sincerely patriotic. He also appreciated the gifts of people from other countries, religions, and cultures, and he was always respectful of and friendly toward the Jewish Poles of Wadowice. It was natural for his sons to learn and project that same attitude. In fact, Lolek's father thought very highly of Jerzy Kluger, Lolek's young Jewish friend. Jerzy would often join Lolek for Mr. Wojtyla's informal class. The boys listened with interest, storing up the knowledge.

Mr. Wojtyla also had a talent for languages. During his army life, he had picked up the languages of some of the surrounding countries. On days when Lolek finished his homework early, his father taught him German. Lolek thought that was fun—and useful, too. Like his father, he enjoyed learning and speaking new languages.

Weather permitting, the Captain and Lolek would follow their light supper with a refreshing walk around town. When they arrived home, the boy would wash and get ready for bed. Every day was a full one, and sleep would come quickly. But before dozing off, he always said his prayers. Mr. Wojtyla knelt beside his own bed each night, deep in silent prayer. Lolek would watch him for as long as he could keep his sleepy eyes open. *I always want to stay close to God, just like my father,* he would think.

Upon waking, the first sight that would meet Lolek's gaze was the peaceful figure of his father, already dressed and kneeling, saying his morning prayers. Lolek's dark eyes would fill with admiration. *I wonder what Papa tells God?* he would muse. *I think he misses Mama, especially now that Mundek is away.*

3

ANOTHER CROSS TO BEAR

"I can't wait until Mundek comes home to visit!" Lolek almost shouted to Jerzy one day. His big brother always had time to play with him and even took him to soccer matches, sometimes hoisting Lolek on his broad shoulders so he could see over the crowd.

Mundek was a good student and did well in medical school. He often spoke to his father and younger brother about the patients who were ill and in need of help. It meant everything to him to become the best doctor he could be. "I want to spend more time with both of you," the young man admitted, "but I just can't do it right now. Someday though, I will. Then we'll all be together again—just the three of us."

Lolek understood that Mundek had to go back to the university for now. He also had to take care of his sick patients. But one day he would live closer to home. *That will be perfect*, the boy decided quietly. *Just perfect*.

When Mundek finally completed medical school in Krakow, he began his practice as a physician in a hospital in the city of Bielsko, much closer to his family. No one was more excited than Lolek, who was now about to enter high school.

Mundek quickly recognized one of his brother's talents. *Lolek loves to perform on stage,* he thought, *and I know the patients at the Bielsko hospital would appreciate some entertainment. It would be great if Lolek could perform for them.*

Lolek was eager to test his acting abilities and readily agreed to do some solo shows at the hospital. He was well-liked, and his performances were a real success. Dr. Wojtyla was glad. He also was grateful that he could make more frequent visits to his family.

The situation was ideal in every way but one. Illnesses that patients brought to the hospital were often contagious. One such illness was Scarlet fever—a high fever accompanied by a skin rash and bright red tongue. The dangerous disease whipped through the wards. Modern medicines, such as antibiotics, were not available back then, and there was no cure for the often-fatal illness.

Mundek and his fellow doctors labored heroically to save their patients. Some doctors, however, contracted the terrible fever. One of them was Mundek. Tragically, Dr. Wojtyla, just

"Jesus, please help Papa and me to be strong."

twenty-six years old and healthy until then, became ill with scarlet fever and died on December 5, 1932.

The Captain and Lolek were stunned and heartbroken. Mundek, like the Captain, had been a role model for twelve-year-old Lolek. This new and unexpected cross was very hard to bear. But father and son consoled each other and found their strength in God and in prayer. Lolek let the hot tears roll down his face. *Jesus, please help Papa and me to be strong now,* he prayed. *Please be with us. Give us your Mother to comfort us.*

Lolek believed that his brother was a real hero because he had given his own life for the good of his patients. It's said that, years later, when Lolek became pope, he kept his brother's stethoscope in the drawer of his desk at the Vatican. It remained Lolek's treasured keepsake.

Lolek's high school years were passing quickly. The teen was serious about his studies and continued cultivating his acting skills. One day, Archbishop Adam Sapieha (*Sa-pee-EH-ha*) came to visit the school. The archbishop was a man of prayer who also held the rank of a Polish prince. Lolek was chosen to give a short welcoming speech for the occasion. He must have been startled when he was told afterward that the archbishop had inquired about him.

"Has young Wojtyla ever thought of the priesthood?" the archbishop asked Father Zacher, the students' chaplain.

"He wants to study philosophy and continue his acting, Your Excellency," Father Zacher answered. "I don't think he feels called to the priesthood."

The archbishop's intense eyes focused on Lolek for a moment. "What a pity," he quietly remarked. "What a pity."

4

Darkening Clouds

Anti-Semitism—discrimination against Jews—was growing in Poland. Some people began to avoid shopping at Jewish-owned businesses. This kind of behavior was promoted by the media, especially by the newspapers, which were, at that time, the main source of information. Certain politicians who were eager for popularity promoted the dangerous trend, too.

Lolek and his friend Jerzy quietly discussed the growing tension in the town. "My father has added his Hebrew name to his office door," Jerzy announced one day. "It's a new law, you know," he added in a nervous whisper.

Lolek drummed his fingers on the arm of his chair. "Where is all this heading, Jerzy?" he asked in frustration. The two friends looked silently at one another. Each dreaded the answer.

One night, not long before their high school graduation, the boys heard a commotion outside. They found out later that some members of an anti-Semitic group had smashed the windows of several Jewish-owned businesses and homes. Lolek and Jerzy went to classes the next day. But they were tense and worried, confused and saddened by the events of the preceding night. Captain Wojtyla must have been anxious, too. That afternoon he was waiting outside the school for Lolek and Jerzy. The Captain greeted Lolek and then hugged Jerzy.

"Please tell your father I send my best regards," Mr. Wojtyla said.

"Thank you, Captain. I will," Jerzy responded with a grateful smile.

Mr. Wojtyla and Lolek walked home. They both felt the need to have a good, long talk. So much was happening; so much was changing.

A short time later, Lolek passed his high school examinations. It was May 14, 1938, just four days before his birthday. The welcome news made him sigh in relief. Now he could set his sights on the famous Jagiellonian (*Yah-gyuh-LOH-nee-on*) University in Krakow.

"I'm looking forward to going to the Jagiellonian soon, Papa," Karol confided to his father. "After all, it was Mundek's school."

"Yes, it was, Lolek. I'll be proud to see you study there too," Mr. Wojtyla encouraged him.

Also in May 1938, Lolek received the sacrament of Confirmation. Shortly afterward, the Wojtylas moved to Krakow and rented an apartment near the large university. Karol was aware there was political turmoil brewing, but he wasn't going to let it stop him. His father had taught him to be brave and to be proud of his country. *I will always be a son of Poland*, he promised himself. *Always*.

Lolek enrolled in literature and philosophy classes. *I love to read, and I enjoy the writings of different countries as well as their languages*, he thought. *I also want to learn about the deeper meaning of life*.

Young Lolek was growing up. At the university, Karol, as he was now called, studied hard, wrote papers, and joined a theater group known as Studio 38. He became associated with a Catholic poetry club, too. Sometimes he read his own poetry at the gatherings. Karol also joined the Society of Mary and made his first pilgrimage to the famous Polish shrine of Our Lady of Czestochowa (*Ches-ta-HO-va*).

His first year at the university passed quickly. Karol was happy with his courses of study, the new friends he had made, and the organizations he had joined. Student life challenged him to grow in his faith in many new and exciting ways. Although he was busy, Karol kept aware of the political situation. An intelligent young man, he could sense trouble brewing . . . trouble on a large scale.

World War I, which had ended in 1918, had left Europe—and indeed the entire world—living under a dark cloud of fear and dread. Many didn't trust the leaders of Germany or the Soviet Union. People wondered whether the uneasy situation would explode into something more tragic and dangerous. They were about to find out.

5

CHANGED FOREVER

September 1, 1939, started out as any other day. Karol, now in his second year at the university, walked briskly to Krakow's Wawel (*VA-vel*) Cathedral. It was the First Friday of the month, and the young man, according to his custom, was on his way to make his confession and serve Mass for his friend and spiritual adviser, Father Figlewicz (*Fee-GLEH-vich*).

Mass began. The familiar Latin prayers were intoned. *In nomine Patris, et Filii, et Spiritus Sancti. Amen.* Suddenly, the interior of the ancient cathedral echoed with a loud, unearthly wail. "What is it?" a visibly shaken elderly woman asked a man kneeling just behind her.

"Air raid siren—" Rapid gunfire and thundering explosions drowned out the reply. People began fleeing in panic. Karol bravely remained by Father Figlewicz's side, and the priest went on with the Mass. As soon as Mass was over, Karol rushed home to reassure himself that his father was all right.

"Go with God, Karol," Father Figlewicz called after him. "And may our Lady protect you!"

The German army had invaded Poland. Krakow's streets were filled with chaos. Within two months, Jagiellonian University was closed and 184 professors were under arrest. Soon schools all around the country were shut down.

Harsh laws were put into place to punish any Poles who resisted the Nazi rule. Food was severely rationed, and clean water was often not available. This ensured that most of the population would soon be too weakened by hunger and disease to resist the cruel occupiers. Museums, theaters, and art galleries were forced to close. In some provinces, the Polish language was banned from use in public offices.

The Nazis are trying to destroy our Polish identity, Karol thought. *We are Poles. It's up to the young people like my friends and me to preserve our culture. Thank God for our Catholic faith. Where else could I find any real joy or hope in this insanity?*

The year 1940 dragged on. In February, Karol met an extraordinary man named Jan (pronounced "Yahn") Tyranowski. A tailor by trade, Mr. Tyranowski stood out as a person of faith in terrible times. He radiated great spiritual strength. This attracted Karol, who admired Mr. Tyranowski's warm devotion to Mary and her Rosary. Jan lived his life in the spirit of the Carmelite religious men and women. This ancient order was dedicated to the Mother of God under the title of Our Lady of Mount Carmel.

Jan soon introduced Karol to the beautiful religious poetry of Saint John of the Cross. Karol was fascinated by the saint, as well as by the life and writings of Saint Teresa of Avila, another famous Carmelite. In his few minutes of free time each day, Karol even started to teach himself Spanish. This would enable him to read the writings of these two great saints in their original language.

Mr. Tyranowski also invited Karol to join the Living Rosary youth group he had started. Karol knew right away that he wanted to be part of such a positive movement.

Healthy young Polish men were being required by the occupying Nazis to take jobs as manual laborers. Any who refused to cooperate would be sent to German work camps— or killed. The new laws forced Karol into hard work in a stone quarry. This job filled many hours each day. When he wasn't working, Karol continued to read and study in secret.

In the midst of all this turmoil, Mr. Wojtyla was growing frail. Karol worried about his father's health. The German's had stopped teh Captain's pension. The small salary that Karol earned was not enough to heat their frigid apartment and put food on the table.

It's up to me, Karol thought. *I have to take care of both of us now.* Before heading home from work at the end of a shift, Karol would scrounge for any scraps of food he could find or buy. A few potatoes and vegetables could make an extra meal and keep them from going hungry. Hurrying back to his apartment, he would whisper his thanks to God for the food in his jacket pocket.

On February 18, 1941, Karol returned home from a long, hard day at the quarry. He could barely feel the tips of his fingers because of the cold. As he often did, he stopped at the neighbors' house to pick up cooked food to take home for the evening meal.

"Papa, I'm home!" Karol called out with enthusiasm. "I'm back." The apartment was unusually quiet.

"Papa," the young man called again, taking quick strides toward the Captain's bedroom. The room was piercingly cold. The elderly man was lying peacefully in bed, wrapped in his thin blankets. Karol stopped in the doorway, shocked. He could see his father wasn't breathing. When he touched the Captain's face and hands, they were as icy as the room. Karol's father was dead.

Karol fell to his knees beside the bed. Silently, tears streamed down his face. He hugged his father's lifeless body. *Please, Lord,* he prayed, *give him eternal rest and peace with you. Please, Lord, take care of him.*

Tearing himself away, Karol ran to nearby Saint Stanislaus Kostka Church. A priest returned with him to anoint Mr. Wojtyla's body. He lingered for a while, trying as best he could to console Karol. After the priest left, Karol continued his prayer vigil alone.

Later, Karol's neighbor Julius Kydrynski came to keep him company. The meal sent by the Kydrynski family remained cold and untouched on the kitchen table. Karol spent that night kneeling at his father's bedside. Once in a while, he spoke a few words to Julius. But mostly, he prayed.

Father Figlewicz celebrated the Captain's funeral Mass. Mr. Wojtyla was buried in the military section of Wadowice's cemetery. Karol was numb—from loneliness as much as from the cold.

After his father's death, Karol did a lot of thinking. He pondered the meaning of life, of

God and the Church, of his own faith, of human suffering, and of Christian love. The more Karol reflected, the more he came to realize what his faith meant to him and the more he came to understand the value of a priestly vocation. *Could God possibly want me to be a priest? Speak, Lord,* he begged. *Please, let me know your will.*

6

DECISION

Days stretched into weeks. Soon it was spring again. On May 18, 1941, Karol turned twenty-one. On his way to work that day, Karol saw worried faces and overheard people talking in hushed tones.

"Have you heard the latest? The Gestapo, the Nazi secret police, dragged the priests right out of the rectory in Wadowice the other day!"

"How could they!" another voice in the crowded market broke in.

"A friend of mine saw them push the priests into cars that were waiting outside. They drove them off as if they were common-criminals . . ."

Young Karol shook his head in disbelief as he heard of more and more injustices being suffered by his fellow Poles. But these new attacks on priests really worried him. *How can we measure the impact of our parish priests on our lives?* Karol reflected. *Without them, we would have no Mass, no sacraments.* The Gestapo had kidnapped the parish priests in the Debniki district of Krakow, too. Karol began to pray even more earnestly.

In October of that year, Karol was transferred to the Solvay chemical plant in the Borek Falecki district of Krakow. The work was hard, but the conditions were a little better than those at the stone quarries. He was even given a cup of soup and a few chunks of bread to eat at noon.

The daily work deadlines set by the Nazis were far beyond what the young workers could reasonably accomplish. The Polish plant managers gave them breaks to lighten the workload, despite their fear of being punished by the occupiers. During those breaks, Karol had time to read, study, think, and pray. In free moments, when his soul needed conversation with God, the young man knelt on the rough stone floor of the factory.

The other plant laborers, husbands and fathers, were decent, hard-working men. Several realized that Karol and his fellow college students found the work heavy and the long hours tedious. These seasoned workers tried to be as considerate and helpful as they could to their younger companions.

Karol Wojtyla never forgot the charity and generosity of so many of his wartime coworkers. Although he could never have imagined it then, one day he, as pope, would write an encyclical letter on the value and dignity of human work.

By the fall of 1942, Karol, with the Lord's help, had made an important decision. Karol walked resolutely to the residence of Archbishop Sapieha in Krakow and knocked on the heavy front door. "I would like to enter the seminary and become a priest," he explained simply to the rector. Karol was warmly welcomed. From that day forward, he began leading a new—and secret—life.

7

GOING UNDERGROUND

Anyone watching Karol at that time would not have noticed any big changes in his life. He still lived in an apartment. He still went to work at the chemical plant every day. And he still did some acting with the theater group he belonged to. But Karol, as an underground seminarian, was living in a new and invisible spiritual world.

Because the Nazis had forbidden the Catholic Church in Poland from accepting any new seminarians, and had arrested and even killed some of the seminarians they found, Archbishop Sapieha had begun a secret, or underground, seminary. The seminarians couldn't let others know that they were preparing to become priests. They had to study during the little free time they had and take their exams in secret. Karol knew the dangers but wasn't worried. He felt in his heart that he was doing what God had in mind for him.

On the evening of February 29, 1944, Karol left the chemical factory and as usual walked quickly toward his apartment. He had worked a double shift. *I'm so tired*, he thought to himself. *I'm ready for some sleep*.

There was quite a bit of traffic, as always. Streetcars crawled their way along the crowded roads. Cars and trucks roared at a brisk wartime pace. Karol looked both ways and stepped into the street. As he began to cross, a German truck seemed to come out of nowhere. It struck him and zoomed ahead. The driver of the large truck, trying to deal with the heavy traffic, probably didn't even realize he had hit someone. Karol, lying unconscious by the side of the road, was soon spattered with mud.

A passenger riding by on a streetcar noticed the body in the dim light. Jumping off the tram, she waved down a passing car for help. A German officer stopped to assist. "Bring some water," he directed, pointing to a nearby ditch. Together the two cleaned the mud from the young man's face. "He's still alive!" the officer exclaimed. "Quickly! Accompany him to the hospital. Please make sure that he's cared for."

"I will," the woman, Mrs. Florek, promised. The officer flagged down a truck and had

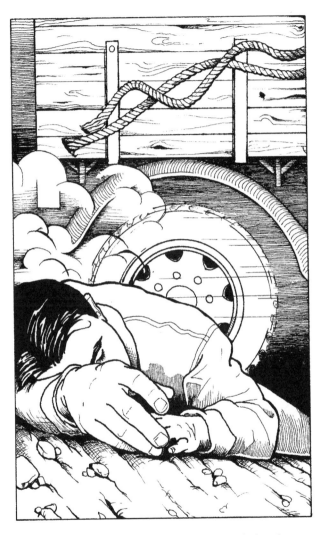

The truck struck Karol and zoomed ahead.

Karol and his guardian transported to the nearest hospital.

Karol woke up in a clean hospital bed. His arm was in a cast and his head was bandaged. He had no idea what day it was. He had suffered a brain injury, cuts, and bruises. Because he was young and vigorous, he was able to recover after two weeks in the hospital. The young seminarian spent his recovery time reflecting on the whole incident. He thought about Mrs. Florek, the helpful German soldier, the strangers who had driven him to the hospital, the wonderful hospital staff. *God bless them all*, Karol thought. *This accident must have happened for a reason. Maybe God wants to convince me of my priestly calling.*

When Karol was released from the hospital, he went right back to his normal life. Full of his usual optimism, he prayed, studied, and worked.

Not long after, in April 1944, one of Karol's friends, a fellow underground seminarian, was arrested and shot by the Gestapo for no known reason. The situation in Krakow was growing more tense and dangerous day by day.

On August 6, 1944, Archbishop Sapieha brought the underground seminarians to his own residence. There they would live and continue their classes secretly. The archbishop sent Father Figlewicz to ask the Polish managers at the Solvay chemical plant if they could start a rumor that Karol had suddenly "disappeared." No information on his real whereabouts could be given to any of the German investigators who would ask why Karol was no longer showing up for work. Those in charge of the plant hesitated at first. But their loyalty and devotion to the Church inspired them to take the risk. Somehow, Karol Wojtyla did indeed soon "disappear," remaining in hiding with his fellow seminarians for the final months of the war.

In January 1945, German troops pulled out of Krakow. But they were making way for new occupiers: the Soviet army. World War II was finally over, but it had been long and cruel. So many of the countries involved in the terrible ordeal were decimated. Poland was no exception. More than seven million Poles had died, at least three million of whom were Jews. In the midst of the turmoil, poverty, and suffering that continued under the Soviets, Karol kept working at his studies. He understood that now, more than ever, Poland would need priests.

Karol was finally ordained on All Saints'
Day, November 1, 1946, by Archbishop—now
Cardinal—Sapieha, in the cardinal's chapel.
He was a priest of God forever! It was a
wonderful day at the cardinal's house.

Just two weeks later, on November 15,
1946, Father Karol Wojtyla left by train for
Rome to begin his graduate theological studies. His thoughts turned to prayer as the train
rocked through parts of Europe he had only
read about in history books.

He and another priest, Father Starowieyski
(*Stah-roh-VEE-EY-skee*) became students at
the well-known Angelicum University run by
the Dominican Order. The two young priests
temporarily took up residence at the nearby
house of the Pallottine Fathers. They began
classes immediately and studied with enthusiasm. Soon, arrangements were made for the
two Polish students to live at the Belgian
College.

On their first Sunday in Rome, the two
friends walked to Saint Peter's Square. They
were just in time to see Pope Pius XII being
carried on his special chair into Saint Peter's
Basilica. Living in Rome was not easy in those
immediate postwar years. The people of Italy
had suffered much in the war, too. But Father
Karol compared life there to the terror and

poverty the Poles were still enduring under the Communist rule of the Soviet Union.

I'm living in freedom now, he thought. *My beloved Poland should be free, too. Everyone has the God-given right to be free. Everyone!*

8

In the Heart of the Church

Living in Rome opened up a new and exciting world to young Father Wojtyla. The ancient city was truly universal and welcomed people from every culture and nation. The Romans were kind, uncomplicated, and positive people. There was a lot to learn from them.

Father Wojtyla loved the musical quality of the Italian language. Even more, he loved the Christian culture that bathed Rome. In this city of Saints Peter and Paul, Karol felt he was at home in the heart of the Catholic Church. Here in Rome he was surrounded by Saint Peter's Basilica, the catacombs, the Coliseum, and beautiful churches and shrines wherever he went. Even at busy street corners carved-out niches in the ancient city walls held small statues or pictures of the Madonna.

Being Catholic in Rome felt as natural as getting up and going to work. *The Italians, too, have suffered the war's effects*, Karol thought, *but now they're moving on*. As he walked, looking into the stores filled with shoppers, he soaked in a sense of optimism—an optimism he would never lose. *God is good,* he thought. *Somehow, this kind of freedom must lie ahead for Poland, too!*

It wasn't long before Father Wojtyla was assigned to help out in one of the city's parishes. Each Sunday, a van dropped him off at the Church of Saint Francis Xavier at around 9:00 AM. Although his Italian language skills still needed improvement, Father Wojtyla made himself available to hear confessions there. In the early afternoon, the van would return to pick him up. Feeling fulfilled in his vocation, Karol would happily rejoin the other priests at the Belgian College.

I love to study and learn, the young man admitted, *but what I find even more rewarding is being among God's people. That's one of the main reasons a man becomes a priest.* Karol was moved by the welcoming spirit he found at Saint Francis Xavier Parish. He could have never foreseen that many years later he would return there for a visit . . . as Pope John Paul II!

Father Wojtyla received his degree in theology on July 3, 1947. That summer, he and his friend, Father Starowieyski, toured France, Belgium, and Holland. Cardinal Sapieha paid for the trip. The cardinal felt this would be a powerful postwar learning experience for his young priests.

Karol visited the town of Ars, France, a living memorial to the great Saint John Marie Vianney, who served there for many years as a parish priest. He also spent time among Polish workers in Charleroi, Belgium. They were grateful to receive the sacraments in their native language.

Soon enough, Karol headed back to Rome to continue his classes at the Angelicum. In June of the following year, 1948, Father Wojtyla completed his classes. But before he could finish his program, he had to write and present to some of his professors a long, scholarly paper called a thesis. The title of his thesis was *The Problems of Faith in the Works of Saint John of the Cross*. Jan Tyranowski, the tailor who had so influenced young Wojtyla, would have been honored to know that Karol had chosen to write on his favorite saint.

The Angelicum required a published thesis before a student could receive his doctoral degree. That was a real problem for Father Wojtyla. He had no money to pay the publication fees. *Something will turn up, for I trust that this is God's plan for me*, he thought. *Perhaps one of my old professors at Jagiellonian University can give me some ideas.*

At the beginning of July, as the relentless Roman sun scorched the city, Father Wojtyla boarded the train to return to Poland. *All I can do*, he prayed in his heart, *is thank you, Jesus, my Lord. Thank you, Mother Mary.* The train swayed rhythmically back and forth. Karol's eyes slowly closed in sleep.

Finally arriving in Krakow, Karol thought how wonderful it would be to see Cardinal Sapieha again. As he walked toward the cardinal's residence, Karol's thoughts also turned to his family. *It's true they can't be here to meet me*, he reflected, *but my family is present in another way. I feel them so near right now. I know they love me and are proud of me. Lord*, he prayed, *grant Mama, Papa, and Mundek eternal rest and peace. I ask them to also pray for me — that I may be a good and holy priest.*

9

Home Again

Back in Poland, Father Wojtyla was first sent to the Church of the Assumption of Our Lady. This country parish was located in Niegowic, a village about fifteen miles from Krakow. Cardinal Sapieha hoped that the kindly pastor, Father Buzala, and the healthy country cooking would help to put a few pounds on the lean young priest.

The old rectory was clean and unadorned. There was no central heating, indoor plumbing, electricity, or hot water. Karol's few belongings easily fit into his small bedroom. Father Wojtyla smiled as he looked around. He whispered a short prayer to Saint John Vianney, the patron saint of parish priests: *I think you'd be at home here. And so am I!*

As Karol was getting acquainted with the parishioners, wonderful news arrived. He would receive his doctoral degree in theology from Jagiellonian University on December 26, 1948. The famous Polish university had accepted his Roman studies and his revised thesis on Saint John of the Cross! Now the twenty-eight-year-old priest could concentrate fully on his parish ministry.

Karol was assigned to the religious education of grade school children in the area. That meant traveling by cart to five schools. Word of the new curate circulated quickly among the parishioners. "He doesn't have anything for himself other than a few books," one observer reported.

"He's just as poor as we are!" a woman broke in. "Have you seen that winter coat he wears? It's so threadbare you can almost see through it."

"And his shoes, they won't last much longer, either," an elderly man added, shaking his head.

"My mother says you're poor—just like us," a little boy confided to Father Wojtyla after religion class one day. Karol grinned broadly. "Thank you," he replied, ruffling the boy's blond hair. "That's a great compliment, you know!"

Day-to-day life in Niegowic was difficult, but also exciting and full of small joys. Father Wojtyla admired the parents' concern for the religious education of their children. And he especially enjoyed his work with the children. "Some are quiet and well-behaved," he noted. "Some are very lively, too!"

In the eight months he spent at the Church of the Assumption of Our Lady, Karol, desiring to imitate Saint John Vianney, dedicated long hours to hearing the confessions of his parishioners. He celebrated thirteen weddings and baptized forty-eight babies. He also started a Living Rosary group and organized parish activities ranging from a play, in which he acted the main role, to discussion groups and sporting events. Father Karol even visited every family in the parish during the Christmas season, adding his rich voice to the happy singing of Polish Christmas carols.

As the people of Niegowic were to learn, Father Karol's dreams were just as big as his heart. When it came time to plan a celebration for the pastor's fiftieth anniversary of priesthood, Karol asked the parishioners, "What can we give Father Buzala as a gift?"

"Maybe we can clean up the parish grounds and plant some new flowers," a young mother suggested.

"And paint that fence around the church," a farmer added.

The young priest thought for a few moments. "This church building has served our parish well for many years," he said quietly. "But don't you think it's time that we build a new one?"

His listeners gasped in surprise. "We have nothing, Father," an elderly parishioner timidly protested. "How can we ever raise enough money to build a church?"

"Don't worry," Karol reassured. "We can do it—if all of us work together. We'll raise the money and build the church ourselves. The Lord will help us. Agreed?"

"Agreed!" the people answered wholeheartedly. "The pastor gets a new church for his fiftieth anniversary!"

And, working together, Father Karol and his parishioners were indeed able to raise the money and get the church built! That red brick church—the first of many that were built because of Father Karol—is still used today. It remains a sign of the miracles that hope and generosity can perform.

10

TO KRAKOW

Cardinal Sapieha had not forgotten young Father Wojtyla. In fact, before the end of his first year at the Church of the Assumption, Karol was called in for a meeting with the prelate.

Cardinal Sapieha listened intently as Father Wojtyla enthusiastically spoke about his parish assignment. "I'm happy to be there," Karol said. "Summed up in one word, I would say it is a *joy*."

"I'm glad," the cardinal responded, nodding his head in approval.

The cardinal is known to be a man of few words, Karol thought. *But they're always the right ones!* "Will I be returning to Niegowic, your Eminence?" he asked.

"No," was the reply. "I have another assignment for you—one that is very important, to my way of thinking."

Karol waited expectantly. "I'm sending you to Saint Florian's Parish," the cardinal continued. "There you will serve as a chaplain to the university students of three of Krakow's schools."

"Well," Father Karol said, "I'll miss Our Lady of the Assumption parish, but this new assignment sounds challenging. I'm happy we'll be able to reach more young people, too."

Karol moved his meager belongings to Saint Florian's. The students and parishioners liked the enthusiastic priest right away. But it was no secret that even some of his most intelligent parishioners were struggling to understand his challenging sermons! Once, Karol asked a professor to tell him honestly how he could improve his sermons. "Could you bring your talks down a few notches and make them more practical?" the man asked with a smile.

"I promise to try," Karol responded with a grin. "Thank you for the good advice."

The young priest worked at becoming constantly more caring and approachable. As he got to know the spiritual needs of his parish, he organized courses for engaged couples. Father Karol taught about respect for the human person and the sacredness of human love. He also taught people to find joy and love in the lifetime commitment of marriage.

"Christian marriage is a beautiful calling that grows and lasts a lifetime," the young priest stressed. His classes swelled. Couples weren't afraid to ask hard questions. Karol responded with helpful information. He encouraged the young people to discuss and share their opinions. Together, the groups would examine individual questions and opinions in the light of Church teaching. Father Karol's marriage preparation courses were a great success.

Saint Florian's young people were attracted to their friendly new priest. Even Father Karol's homilies were growing on them. Whenever Karol used words that weren't part of their vocabulary, the students would jot them down and check their dictionaries later!

"I'd like to start a student choir," Karol announced one day. "If you're interested, please join me in the choir loft on the evening of Candlemas Day, February 2, the last day for singing Christmas carols."

Karol was the first to arrive. Each student, at the end of the climb to the choir loft, was met with the priest's welcoming smile and warm handshake. Karol intoned the carols and their hearts lightened. This new priest could really sing! Many of the young people stopped singing and just listened. They felt themselves relaxing. The fears and worries of life under a Communist government seemed far away.

As they were saying goodbye, Father Karol made an announcement. "Just one last thing. I'd like to invite any of you who are interested to come to my 6:00 AM Mass on Wednesday."

"Thanks, Father," someone said. "I'll let you know."

"I'll think about it," another student replied.

"Six in the morning," mumbled a third, shaking his head. "Too early for me . . ."

Karol followed the last student back into the main part of the church. Approaching the altar rail, he knelt and prayed a long time before returning to the rectory that night. *I wonder if any of them will really come*, he mused. *I wonder . . .*

11

Uncle Karol

To Karol's great surprise and joy, several of the students *did* begin to attend his early morning Masses. Little by little, Father Karol introduced them to an ancient form of Church music called Gregorian chant. On Saint Florian's feast day in 1951, the student choir sang the beautiful *Mass of the Angels* for the first time.

A small group of college students also began to gather around Father Karol at Saint Florian's church for prayer, socializing, conferences, and discussions. Since they felt like a close-knit family, the young people began calling themselves Rodzinka (*Roh-JIN-kah*), the Polish word for "little family."

Because Poland's Communist government had forbidden priests to work with youth groups, Karol could not openly show that he was a priest when he was with the students, except at Mass. "You can't call me 'Father' in public, either," Karol warned.

"Then what should we call you? You're too young to be a *grandfather*!" someone quipped. They all laughed.

"What if you call me 'Uncle'?" Karol suggested.

Uncle, or Wujek (*VOO-yek*) in Polish, was perfect. So Uncle Karol it was.

Even though it was practically unheard-of in those days—not to mention against the law—for a priest to go on vacation with a group of young people and married couples, Father Wojtyla paid no attention. In the winter, he and his friends packed their skis for trips to the mountains. "Uncle" loved to ski and was very good at it.

Karol felt full of life and energy as he sped down the shimmering slopes against the rush of the icy wind. Glancing back, he could see that his exuberant young friends were also caught up in the magic of the moment. *Thank you, Lord, for the beauty of your creation*, he silently prayed, *and for the beauty of human friendship and love*. As the years passed, several married couples began bringing their entire families along on these vacation trips.

During the summer months, hiking and camping drew Father Wojtyla and his friends together. One of Karol's young friends, Jurek Ciesielski, was a certified teacher of kayaking.

Always ready to learn, Karol was soon paddling his own kayak down Poland's lakes and rivers.

The clean mountain air refreshed everyone. Each day began with Father Wojtyla's celebration of an outdoor Mass. An upside-down kayak served as an altar, while two paddles tied together formed a large cross. "Uncle" also enjoyed singing and telling stories with the group.

Breakfast was prepared over campfires. Everyone ate heartily and joined in the cleanup. Then the day's events were announced. "Uncle," one of the young students shyly whispered one day, "could I speak with you when you have a few minutes? I could use some advice."

"How about joining me this afternoon on our trip down the river?" Father Wojtyla responded with a grin. "My kayak has room for two."

Many of the young people teamed up with Uncle in his kayak on other days. Some asked for counseling. Others just needed a listening heart. Still others made their confessions.

For all the fun, jokes, and stories they shared, the young people also understood Father Wojtyla's need for solitude. They never objected when he purposely fell back to the

"Uncle" Karol used his kayak as a place
to hear confessions or offer advice.

end of the group of hikers to pray in silence along the trail. There was so much to talk to the Lord about!

The days of hiking and camping were wonderful, but also long and tiring. Even the prickly straw that served as the campers' mattresses at night looked inviting as cool air blanketed the slopes. Feeling the ache of sore muscles, one of the young men joked one night, "'Uncle,' when you're pope some day, will you at least give us blessings for walking this steep trail in the dark?"

Karol threw back his head and laughed. Him, pope? What a ridiculous idea!

12

POLAND'S YOUNGEST BISHOP

Communist government officials kept a close eye on Father Wojtyla, as they did on all Catholic priests. "This one's nothing but a scholar, an actor, an idealistic poet," the authorities assured one another. "As long as he doesn't spread his teachings, he shouldn't cause us problems." Little did they know how wrong they were. They had no idea what a great effect "Uncle" Karol was secretly having on hundreds of young people!

Cardinal Sapieha died at the age of eighty-four on July 23, 1951. He was buried in Wawel Cathedral. This great man had a lasting influence on Father Wojtyla. After all, he had welcomed Karol to his underground seminary during World War II, and he had ordained him. Karol felt deeply the loss of this spiritual leader who had bravely stood up to the Nazis in defense of his Church and country.

Archbishop Eugene Baziak became the new archbishop of Krakow, even though the Communist Polish government refused to acknowledge him. The archbishop sent Father

Wojtyla for further studies that would qualify him as a university professor. Everything went well, and Karol began to teach. His classes were popular.

"I'm happy that you listen to me," Karol smilingly acknowledged to his students one day. "Don't forget, though—I want to hear from you, too. I want your input. It's never wrong to bring up questions, or to ask me to explain things more clearly."

After a few classes, Karol's students relaxed. They began sharing what was in their hearts and on their minds. Among Karol's many students was Stanislaw Dziwisz (*GEE-vish*), a young man studying for the priesthood. Father Wojtyla taught him for six years and was impressed by his many good qualities.

Stanislaw was eventually ordained and assigned to a parish. A few years later, Father Stanislaw was sent for further studies in Church liturgy. He could never have dreamed that someday Karol Wojtyla would become a cardinal and then pope—and that *he* would become his secretary!

On July 4, 1958, Karol, then only thirty-eight years old, was named a bishop by Pope

Pius XII. It was the last official appointment that Pope Pius made before his death. Father Wojtyla was consecrated an auxiliary bishop by Archbishop Baziak on September 28, 1958, becoming the youngest bishop in Poland. He chose as his motto the Latin words *"Totus Tuus"* (*toe-tus too-us,*) which means "entirely yours." This motto was an expression of Karol's lifelong devotion to Mary, the Mother of God.

At the beginning of the next year, on January 25, 1959, the newly elected Pope John XXIII startled everyone by announcing that he was going to call an important worldwide Church meeting in Rome. The Second Vatican Council was scheduled to begin in October 1962, but Archbishop Baziak died in June of that year.

Later in June, Bishop Wojtyla substituted for the deceased archbishop and ordained the archdiocese's new priests. Karol was then named temporary leader of the archdiocese of Krakow until a new archbishop could be appointed by Rome.

Then trouble began. Local Polish government officials suddenly announced that they were taking over a seminary building for their own purposes. Bishop Wojtyla was informed of the plan. Without an invitation, he appeared at the government headquarters.

"I'd like to have a brief meeting with the people in charge here," he respectfully explained. He waited only a few moments before being led into a room where the appropriate officials had hastily gathered. The secretary who had led him in left quickly, closing the door with a faint trace of a smile.

The meeting was short, cordial, and to the point. The outcome was this: the seminary would keep control of the first two floors of the building while the remaining third floor would be used by the government until it could find another suitable location. Krakow's government learned then and there that the new bishop was not afraid to defend the rights of his people and his Church.

Bishop Wojtyla was enthusiastic about the upcoming Second Vatican Council. "I believe it will bring a great and powerful renewal of our Church for the whole world," he explained to his staff and friends. "Jesus' message needs to be presented with originality for every generation, in every circumstance. Imagine what the Council will mean for those of us living in Communist countries! We'll be able to meet other bishops from around the world and share our experiences. The Holy Spirit will come among us with his truth and love. It will be like a new Pentecost!"

13

A MIRACLE ...
AND BACK TO ROME

Bishop Wojtyla had a few urgent matters to clear up before he left for Rome and the Council meetings. The first concerned his friend Dr. Wanda Poltawska. The psychiatrist was a young wife and mother who had been diagnosed with a very serious cancer. Karol felt the concern and sorrow of Wanda and her husband and family.

"What about my children, and my husband and patients?" the doctor had confided to Bishop Wojtyla, "I want to be brave, Uncle, but I need strength from God. I need a miracle!"

"I will pray for you," Karol had promised. "I will pray with all my heart."

Bishop Wojtyla sat at his desk, thinking deeply. An inspiration came. He picked up his pen and drew out a clean sheet of paper. His eyes glistened as he began a letter to Padre Pio, a Franciscan Capuchin friar in Italy. Padre Pio was becoming famous for his holiness; he actually bore the *stigmata*, wounds like those of Jesus, on his body. Many people asked him to hear their confessions and to pray for their health. Here is what Karol wrote:

Dear Padre Pio, I want to ask you for your prayers. One of my dear friends, Dr. Wanda Poltawska, has been diagnosed with terminal cancer. Will you please intercede with the Lord for her complete cure? I trust in your prayers.

Padre Pio's answer wasn't long in coming: Yes, he would pray for Wanda.

Dr. Poltawska was scheduled for her surgery. She arrived at the hospital for the routine tests that would precede the operation. To the amazement of the doctors, the X-rays clearly showed that the large, cancerous tumor had completely disappeared!

Bishop Wojtyla understood that Wanda had been cured. He knew, without a doubt, that God had worked a miracle through Padre Pio, the humble friar. Who could have guessed that someday Karol Wojtyla, as pope, would have the privilege of beatifying and canonizing him? Padre Pio would be declared blessed on May 2, 1999, and named a saint on June 16, 2002.

The most pressing matters having been taken care of, Krakow's young bishop was ready to leave for Rome. He celebrated Mass with many of his priests and people, praying for the success of Pope John XXIII's world council. On the evening of October 5, 1962, Bishop Wojtyla traveled by train to Rome.

The Second Vatican Council, gentle Pope John XXIII explained, was to be a *pastoral* council. The word "pastoral" refers to concern for Jesus' flock, the people who make up his Church. Most councils in the past had been *doctrinal*, focusing on what we as a Church believe. However, the new council's focus would also prove to be very important. It would be concerned with the spiritual and material needs of all the people of God. Pope John was greatly loved by Catholics all over the world. They heard him speak and watched him, too, on small black-and-white television screens.

The pope blessed all the participants of the council, and the sessions began on October 11, 1962. Bishops from all over the world participated. Bishop Wojtyla attended every session of the Second Vatican Council. It was an experience he would never forget.

Important meetings and speeches filled the Council hall. The Council Fathers reflected on the Church, on praying and working in the modern world. They listened with all their hearts to the Holy Spirit, as the first Christians had done. It was now time to go back to the beginnings of the Church, to the roots of Catholicism.

When the Council Fathers wished to speak about various topics, they signed up and took turns addressing the large assembly. Bishop Wojtyla spoke to the Council about suggested changes to the Church's liturgy. These changes affected how Catholics prayed and worshipped God. Karol also contributed to a discussion on what Catholics believe as being divinely revealed by God.

Days and months passed as the Council met. But June 1963 brought a sorrowful turn of events. Pope John XXIII was very ill. People began to gather under his window at the Vatican. They prayed the Rosary and other prayers for him. The pope was dying of stomach cancer. He entered eternal life on June 3, 1963. People everywhere showed their love and respect for the gentle, smiling pope.

Pope John didn't live to complete the great Council that was so close to his heart. From heaven, though, he would still be present. The important work would go on.

The cardinals gathered in a special meeting, called a conclave, to choose a new pope. White smoke puffed from the chimney of the

Sistine Chapel on June 21. This was the signal that a new pope had been elected! He was Cardinal John Baptist Montini of Milan, Italy. He chose the name Pope Paul VI.

The Council's work continued. There would be four sessions in all. During the remainder of the sessions, some important things happened to Bishop Wojtyla. First, with a group of other bishops, he went on a ten-day pilgrimage to the Holy Land, the place where Jesus walked and talked, performed miracles, died, and rose from the dead. Then Karol returned to Rome. He worked with his fellow bishops on important documents, such as *The Church in the Modern World*, and contributed to an explanation of the role of lay people in the life of the Catholic Church.

On December 30, 1963, Paul VI named Karol as Archbishop of Krakow. The people of Krakow rejoiced. Although his participation in the Vatican Council required him to remain temporarily in Rome, Archbishop Wojtyla's heart was yearning for Poland, his native land.

Karol Wojtyla was consecrated archbishop on March 8, 1964. He celebrated the joyful event by taking part in another two-week pilgrimage to the Holy Land. Soon the Second Vatican Council was underway again, and he returned to Rome. Archbishop Wojtyla continued to visit his people in Krakow as often as he could. He explained the important work of the Council in his homilies at Mass. He made his Polish people feel part of it all.

14

SURPRISE REUNION

Twenty years had passed since the end of World War II. Two childhood friends from Wadowice had lost track of each other over the years. It would have been logical for each to believe that the other hadn't survived the horrible war. But that was about to change.

Jerzy Kluger, now a prominent engineer living in Rome, opened his newspaper one morning. He quickly skimmed the articles, as he did every day. A story about a talk given at the Vatican Council suddenly caught his eye. To be more specific, a *name* mentioned in the article seemed to jump off the page—the name Karol Wojtyla. *Interesting,* the Jewish engineer mused. *Wojtyla isn't that common a name. Could it possibly be Lolek after all these years?* He sat staring at the article for a few minutes. *Well, it wouldn't hurt to check it out.*

Reaching for the phone, Mr. Kluger dialed the Polish Institute in Rome. He was told that Archbishop Wojtyla was indeed staying there during the Council, but was out at the moment.

Jerzy left a message, asking the archbishop to call him back. Karol returned the call as soon as he got home.

"Jerzy?" Karol asked in amazement.

"Karol?" Jerzy almost shouted with joy.

"Yes, it's me, Jerzy!" Karol cried. "Can you come right over?"

"I'll be there in a few minutes!" Jerzy shot back. He hung up and was soon on his way. The Roman traffic was moving at a snail's pace. Jerzy struggled to keep calm as he negotiated his way through a sea of motorcycles, cars, and pedestrians. He kept hearing the voice on the phone: It was Lolek, his best friend. Lolek! How many years it had been since he had seen him!

After finding a parking place, he was invited into a parlor of the Polish Institute to await the archbishop. But there was no wait. Almost immediately, Karol appeared at the top of the staircase. His face lit up when he spotted Jerzy. Rushing down the stairs, Karol headed straight for his friend. The two men stood speechless for a moment. Then they joyfully embraced. "It's so good to see you, Karol . . . but, ah, what am I supposed to call you now?" the Jewish man asked respectfully. "Should I say 'Your Excellency'?"

"Just call me Lolek!"

"Oh, Jerzy," Karol grinned back, "just call me Lolek!" The two men sat down and had a wonderful conversation. There was so much to catch up on. So many miles, events, and years to share!

The fourth and final session of the Second Vatican Council ended on December 8, 1965.

Karol was anxious to get back to Krakow. There he immediately set to work introducing his people to the sixteen documents issued by the Second Vatican Council. He wanted all his people—both religious and laity—to study and to deepen the treasures of the Council. He wanted all to find peace and hope in their Catholic faith.

On June 28, 1967, Pope Paul VI named Karol a cardinal. Cardinal Wojtyla kept himself very busy. Besides his work with his priests and people, he published books that were eventually translated from Polish into many different languages, including English. They were books that explored profound truths about God and human beings. Karol wanted people to know about God's goodness and to believe more deeply in his great love for us.

Cardinal Wojtyla soon consecrated two auxiliary bishops who became his helpers. It was a good thing, because Karol had *many* projects in mind.

15

A Shepherd's Heart

One of Karol's special projects was a pilgrimage to Rome, which lasted from May 22 until June 2, 1970. The pilgrims were all Polish priests who had been prisoners of the Nazis in Dachau, Germany. It was a very moving experience for them to travel to the Eternal City with their cardinal.

Dachau's Nazi concentration camp in southern Germany included a building called the "priests' block." More than 2,500 priests were held prisoners there during the war. A great number of them were Polish. It is recorded that of the 1,780 Polish priests, only 912 survived.

The terrible concentration camp was liberated by the U.S. Army on April 29, 1945. Now, twenty-five years later, the heroic priests who were physically able to make the trip were reunited during their pilgrimage to Rome.

Cardinal Wojtyla's eyes shone with tears of respect and love as he listened to Pope Paul warmly greet the priests. *As difficult as my life was during the war, especially after having lost my father, my own sufferings seem small compared with what these brave apostles of Christ suffered,* Karol thought. *I'm happy to be able to provide them with the consolation of this pilgrimage. They deserve it.*

Back in Krakow, Cardinal Wojtyla visited the parishes of his diocese. He was caring and unrushed. This energetic man had a clear grasp of the importance of life and the meaning of time. He would stay in a parish as long as necessary, even if it meant several weeks. He took on the various tasks of the parish priests. He wanted to experience for himself the positive and negative challenges of their ministry. He realized that being a parish priest in a country where the people were not free to openly worship God involved special hardships.

Karol also wanted to make sure the children of Krakow were being instructed in their Catholic faith. *Even though the authorities won't allow me to visit them in their schools,* the cardinal reasoned, *they can't stop me from meeting the children during their parish religious instruction classes.* And that's exactly what he did!

"Sometimes," a pastor explained to him, "we priests have to take over teaching the religion classes because the volunteer parishioners are afraid to come. If the government officials catch them, they can lose their jobs. And they need those jobs to support their families."

Cardinal Wojtyla rubbed his chin thoughtfully. "It's true," he quietly answered. "Our nation is still in chains." *Please, Lord,* he silently prayed, *give us Polish people the joy of someday being able to love and serve you as a free nation.*

The time the cardinal spent in his parishes taught him many new and practical ways to bring the Catholic faith into the lives of his people. Because he had been privileged to attend the sessions of the Second Vatican Council, he felt enriched by the new opportunities that were unfolding for the worldwide Church. These were challenging but rewarding times to be alive and to shepherd God's people. Still, Karol had no way of foreseeing just *how* challenging his life would soon become.

Pope Paul VI, who had completed the Vatican Council begun by Pope John XXIII, became ill. He died on August 6, 1978. It was the feast of the Transfiguration. Karol received the sad news in Poland. He had highly esteemed Pope Paul, especially for his heroic defense of the sacredness of all human life, from the instant of conception in each mother's womb until the moment of natural death. Karol immediately went to his private chapel. He remained there a long time in quiet prayer.

Cardinal Wojtyla was soon on his way back to Rome, this time to attend Pope Paul's funeral and to participate in the conclave that would elect the new pope.

On August 25, 1978, the Catholic world rejoiced in the announcement that a new pope had been elected. He was Cardinal Albino Luciani from Naples, Italy. People were thrilled to have such a warm and approachable man chosen as the successor of Saint Peter. Cardinal Luciani chose to be named after the two popes who had come before him. He took the name John Paul I.

Cardinal Wojtyla and the other cardinals were pleased. They thanked the Holy Spirit for having enlightened them in their voting. Karol returned to Poland with a joyful heart. He knew that the Church was in good hands.

Nearly a month later, Karol had just finished celebrating morning Mass. He was having his breakfast when unbelievable news arrived. . . The pope was dead! Pope John Paul I had passed away unexpectedly during the night.

Karol was shocked. Leaving his breakfast behind, he headed straight for his chapel. *What does this all mean, Lord?* he prayed. *A pope for only thirty-three days! What is your will for the Church now? Please, Lord, what is your will?*

FROM A FARAWAY COUNTRY

As he once more packed his bags for Rome, Cardinal Wojtyla was deep in thought. It seemed impossible that he was returning to Italy so soon. He would be taking part in John Paul's funeral. The conclave to choose the next pope would follow. Karol remembered the cardinals from the previous meeting. He had gotten to know several of them. They passed silently through his mind now. *I pray especially* he whispered, *for the man who will accept the heavy burden of walking in the footsteps of Saint Peter. I beg you, Lord, give him all the graces he will need.*

Before leaving for Rome, Karol celebrated a Mass for Pope John Paul I. His homily came straight from his heart. "Why did this happen?" he asked the worshippers. "What does this pope's death mean for the whole Church? We don't know what Jesus is telling us through this event. But we trust him."

The conclave to elect the new pope began on October 14, 1978. October 15 found black smoke spouting from the little stove in the

Sistine Chapel. The waiting world understood the signal—no pope had yet been chosen. On Monday, October 16, a new climate seemed to stir among the cardinals. Karol had remained calm and composed throughout the meetings and discussions. He prayed even more than usual. So much was going through his mind.

His friend Cardinal Konig came to speak with him. What he had to say was incredible! "Karol," the elder cardinal encouraged, "if *you* are elected pope, you must accept. It will be the will of God." What was Karol's reaction to this startling development? He kept his thoughts to himself, even when his mentor, Cardinal Wyszynski (*Vih-SHIN-ski*) encouraged him in the same way.

The voting was moving slowly, but too quickly for Karol. The second voting session of the afternoon of October 16 was held. Each cardinal's name was read aloud from the ballots before the whole assembly. Karol heard his name read ninety-nine times! He struggled to keep calm. The final tally was made. Karol Wojtyla had been elected pope!

Placing all his trust in God and in the help of the Blessed Virgin Mary, Karol humbly accepted. "I will take the same name as Cardinal Luciani," he said simply. "I will be called John Paul II."

John Paul was quickly dressed in his new white cassock and cap. Each cardinal, in turn, came up to pay his respects and offer his allegiance to this brave man who had taken on an awesome responsibility.

Meanwhile, the stove in the Sistine Chapel shot thick clouds of white smoke into the Roman sky. Everyone—those waiting in Saint Peter's Square and the millions around the world watching the event on television—knew what that signal meant. The Catholic Church had a pope once more! The tremendous crowd in the square broke into thunderous cheers. All eyes were riveted on the balcony of Saint Peter's Basilica. The new pope would soon emerge to meet his people.

The impatient spectators didn't have long to wait. Cardinal Pericle Felici appeared on the balcony. "We have a new pope," he solemnly announced in Latin. The crowd clapped and cheered. A suspenseful silence followed. The cardinal continued, "His name is Karol Jozef Wojtyla."

As the people clapped again, a murmur ran through the crowd. Whispers of "Who is he?" "I've never heard his name." "Is he from Africa?" came from every side.

A Polish priest standing near the gate of Saint Peter's Basilica felt as if he had been struck by a thunderbolt. Father Stanislaw Dziwisz exclaimed to no one in particular, "That's my cardinal! *My* cardinal!" Someone who recognized him as Karol's secretary quickly ushered him toward the Basilica.

The new pope understood that the people would not recognize his name. He was very sensitive to the Italian community that had loved John Paul I so much. Karol wanted to make the transition as easy as possible. He quickly stepped up to the microphone and, breaking with custom, introduced himself to his new diocese of Rome. Karol's voice was deep and gentle as his first words, spoken in fluent Italian, filled Vatican Square.

"Praised be Jesus Christ!" he began, using a familiar expression of greeting. The crowd clapped and cheered. "We are all sad about losing our beloved John Paul I," he continued. "Now the cardinals have chosen a new bishop of Rome. They have called someone from a country far away. Far, yes, but near because it is united in our faith. I asked Jesus and his mother, the Madonna, to help me as your pope. I don't know if I am making myself clear in your . . . *our* . . . Italian language."

Even louder cheers filled the square. Pope John Paul II had just embarked on one of the

"Praised be Jesus Christ!"

longest papacies in the history of the Catholic Church.

The crowds at Saint Peter's slowly drifted away. The people had met their new pope. They had heard his message and received his blessing. The long wait had been worth it.

Father Stanislaw, Karol's secretary, was finally led into the dining room where all the cardinals had gathered. *His* cardinal was at the head of the table, dressed completely in white. The priest stared, frozen to the spot. "Pope John Paul II caught my gaze," he recalled later. "It was as if he had bored a hole in my heart. Then he smiled and continued eating. I realized that I was now in the presence of the pope."

The news of Karol Wojtyla's election reached Poland and spread like a raging fire. Church bells rang throughout the land. In Krakow, many of Karol's longtime friends were marveling. Unbelievable as it seemed, "Uncle" was now the pope! Karol's friend Stanislaw Rybicki remarked in awe, "Imagine! He's gone from a kayak to the ship of Peter!"

Not everyone in Poland was celebrating. The Communist authorities were in shock.

17

On the Move

The Vatican personnel who planned the pope's daily schedule of events soon had some adjusting to do. Heads of states as well as diplomats arrived each day to pay their respects, but now personal guests were also invited to visit the pope. John Paul made sure of that! The pope was delighted when Jerzy Kluger, his close childhood friend, came to call with his wife and children. Other good friends stopped by the Vatican as well.

Pope John Paul II was healthy and energetic. He wasn't content with having people come to see him at the Vatican. He wanted to be able to go to them. By the end of his first month as pope, John Paul was ready to burst the bonds of his new Vatican home. He had made up his mind. *The pastor will go to the people,* he decided quietly but firmly. *And why not?* The pope flew by helicopter to the Italian Marian shrine of Mentorella. Word spread almost magically. A huge crowd formed at the shrine and on the surrounding grounds.

"I apologize for the inconvenience," the pope smilingly told the priests who staffed the shrine. "I used to pray here when I was a young priest studying in Rome. And I've come here today to pray." With that simple explanation, he invited the waiting crowd to join him in worshipping the Lord and honoring his mother, Mary.

On November 5, 1978, John Paul made another short trip. That day, he spent time at the famous shrines of Saint Francis in Assisi and Saint Catherine in Siena. Both saints had made a powerful impact on the people of their time. The pope prayed to them for strength and guidance in leading and serving the people of God.

John Paul II was testing his wings. It would take some getting used to for Vatican officials. They had their established way of doing things and of managing the day-to-day affairs of popes. John Paul II, they would soon find out, was now taking the lead, and was usually several steps—or helicopter flights—ahead of them!

One morning, as he was going through his mail, John Paul came across a letter from the Mexican bishops. He opened it and read it carefully. It was an invitation to visit Mexico.

The pope nodded. *Mexico is an oppressed country*, he thought. *I know what oppression is like. Poland, too, is suffering. Besides, if I can actually enter Mexico, it may pave the way for my first trip to Poland.*

The invitation was accepted, and soon plans were underway for the historic papal visit. The pope's plane landed safely in Mexico City on January 26, 1979. Crowds were everywhere. All wanted a glimpse of the man dressed in white. People came seeking a word, a blessing, a smile. And they weren't disappointed. The Mexicans coined a chant that would become famous: *John Paul Two, we love you!* The pope would hear those words wherever he went for the rest of his life.

But Mexico was only the beginning. Everywhere he went, John Paul brought blessings, joy, and hope.

On October 1, 1979, a crowd of two million blanketed Boston Common. Standing space was at a premium. The dampness chilled the crowds to the bone, but no one complained— not even when the rain began to fall, relentlessly pelting the spectators for hours on end. People huddled together and held out their umbrellas for strangers to share. It all seemed so natural.

The ground soon turned to mud, and those without boots sank into the mire. Still they waited in expectation. No one left.

Pope John Paul II arrived to celebrate Mass on a beautiful stage that had been built for the occasion. Time seemed to stop. Although he was partially protected by overhead awnings, he got wet because of the strong winds. His deep voice came over the loudspeaker, booming above the din of the wind and rain. The people responded with joy and enthusiasm.

The impressive Eucharistic celebration drew to a close. But the pope's words—especially his thoughts on the Gospel story of the rich young man Jesus invited to follow him—remained engraved in the crowd's memory. Pope John Paul spoke to each person in the huge assembly that day. "Jesus still passes by," he said. "He still invites young people to follow in his footsteps."

The moment arrived for the pope to leave. The crowd waved and cheered, and finally—reluctantly—began to break up. As a group of nuns headed toward the parking lot, a young man approached one of them. "Sister," he said, "do you have a minute?" The nun looked up from under her rain-soaked veil. The young stranger was just as wet. "Of course," she said with a smile

"I know I can tell a nun," he continued, "and I know you'll share my joy with me. As I walked down the street earlier, the pope passed by in his special car. And he looked at me, Sister. He smiled directly at me and waved. I smiled and waved back, and I knew what I had to do. I had to go to confession. It had been a long time, you know. So I walked over to Saint Anthony's Shrine and made my peace with God. I'm so happy and peaceful now, Sister. That's the gift Pope John Paul gave me today. I just had to tell somebody about it. Thanks a lot, Sister. Please remember to pray for me, and keep thanking God for me, too!"

18

SECRET ESCAPE!

"You know, Stanislaw, I really miss the mountains," Pope John Paul confided to his secretary one day. "After all, I've skied ever since I was a boy. The air is much fresher in the mountains. Skiing is so healthy."

"Do you want to go skiing, Your Holiness?" Father Stanislaw replied. "I mean, really?" The priest's eyes searched the pope's face. Yes, he could see it. John Paul wasn't just reminiscing about the past. He certainly *did* want to go skiing. And he wanted to go without any publicity, fuss, or ceremony. Father Stanislaw grew thoughtful. How could he make this work?

It took a bit of time, but the arrangements were made. The day planned for the papal escape was set: January 2, 1981. Father Tadeusz and Father Joseph would accompany John Paul and Father Stanislaw. The little group's destination was Ovindoli, a little Italian village in the Apennine Mountains. The four friends would be out of the Vatican by nine in the morning, eat their packed lunch in the mountains, and be home for a late supper.

All went according to their plan. Father Joseph drove the black car, and Father Tadeusz sat in the front passenger seat. The pope and Father Stanislaw sat in the back. Father Tadeusz pretended to be reading a newspaper, which he held wide open to hide the pope as the car exited the Vatican—right under the unseeing eyes of the Swiss Guards!

"Why are we going so slowly?" one of the priests asked Father Joseph. "We're never going to get there at this rate."

"I have to be careful," the driver replied with a smile. "After all, I have the pope in the car! Imagine if I got caught speeding or going through a red light." Everyone laughed, and Father Joseph continued cautiously down the open road.

They finally arrived at the ski slopes and got out of the car. It was exciting, especially for the pope. It felt so good to be back in his ski gear again! His eyes shone with joy behind his protective goggles. Out on the crystal slopes John Paul could just be Karol again. It was invigorating and calming, and it made him feel very close to God.

Over the years, the pope and his friends were able to make more than a hundred day trips to the mountains. But one day, John Paul was finally discovered. There he was in his ski clothing and equipment, a perfect disguise, but not perfect enough. A ten-year-old boy who had been skiing with his father and friends wandered a little too far from his group. Suddenly he found himself looking up at a smiling man on skis. "Papa, Papa!" he yelled as loudly as he could. "Come quick! It's the pope!"

John Paul didn't dare speak. That would have been a sure giveaway. One of the pope's companions tried to send the boy back to his family and friends. But the boy stood his ground. So the priests rushed the pope back to their car and jumped in. They made a quick escape. But the secret was out. *The pope skis!*

People thought it was wonderful. The Italian government, however, wanted to guarantee John Paul's safety. They insisted that all future papal ski excursions be accompanied by a police car and a fire truck. From then on, the Swiss Guards stood at attention each time the squad car, the fire truck, and the black van carrying Pope John Paul, three priests, and the pope's butler headed for the slopes.

19

ALL TO ALL

Pope John Paul's familiar white-robed figure became more and more visible through-out the world as the years passed. From 1979 through 2004, he made more than 200 trips outside Italy. He traveled always as a missionary of peace and love in the name of Jesus. In the more than twenty-six years of his papacy—the third longest in 2,000 years (the longest reigning Pope was Saint Peter; the second longest was Blessed Pius IX)—John Paul II visited 129 countries. He traveled more than 700,000 miles, nearly three times the distance between the earth and the moon, or twenty-eight times around the entire earth!

These papal visits included seven to the United States and three to Canada. People in parts of the world where Pope John Paul could not travel could usually watch and listen to him on television. It's no exaggeration to say that John Paul II was probably the most visible and well-known human being in the world during his lifetime. The countries that didn't live in freedom and whose people weren't allowed to watch the pope on television missed a great opportunity. But they were in the pope's prayers. His spiritual boundaries were those of the whole world.

Some people feared for John Paul II's safety as he traveled around the world. Although he had many admirers, there were also those who opposed him and the Gospel values he stood for. All the countries he visited made sure that the pope, a guest in their land, was well protected. It was an honor to have such an important religious person among them.

Strangely enough, the attempt to assassinate Pope John Paul didn't take place in a foreign country. It happened right in Vatican Square. One person in a vast throng of excited, happy people came that day with the intention of killing the pope.

It was Wednesday, May 13, 1981.

A man named Ali Agca aimed his gun and shot twice. The pope, riding around the square in his open-air jeep, fell backward onto his faithful secretary, Father Stanislaw. Blood bathed John Paul's white cassock. Father Stanislaw was stunned. How could this be happening? It was like a horrible nightmare. He cradled the pope in his arms.

"Are you badly hurt, Holy Father?" the priest asked.

"Yes," the pope managed to answer. John Paul remained serene, praying quietly as all around him became chaos, and police and ambulance sirens wailed.

Pope John Paul was taken to the Vatican first-aid station and then rushed to Gemelli Hospital's emergency room. He was gravely injured and underwent immediate surgery. Meanwhile, people all over the world, still in shock over the terrible news, prayed for the Holy Father's recovery.

Pope John Paul did recover, little by little. "It was the Blessed Mother who saved and protected me," he later told the crowds. In fact, May 13, the day Pope John Paul was shot, was the feast of Our Lady of Fatima, the anniversary of the day on which the Blessed Mother appeared to three shepherd children in Fatima, Portugal.

The pope thanked our Mother, Mary, and explained, "The hand of the assassin pulled the trigger, but the hand of Mary directed the bullet and spared my life." Two years later, Pope John Paul, in the spirit of Jesus, visited Ali Agca in prison and forgave him for trying to kill him.

Over the long years of his papacy, Pope John Paul continued his writing. He wrote fourteen special letters called *encyclicals*. These were instructions on such important topics as Jesus our Savior, the Holy Spirit, God's mercy, human work, and Mary. He wrote other documents and letters as well. John Paul was a teacher whose classroom was the whole world. Throughout long days and even into the night, he carried out the Lord's work. In his early years as pope, he usually slept only about four hours a night. The rest of the time was spent in prayer and work.

One of the most important encyclicals written by Pope John Paul II is called *The Gospel of Life*. It emphasizes the Church's belief in the sacredness of all human life. Each individual, before and after birth, is unique and very precious to God. A person, from the moment he or she is conceived in his or her mother's womb until his or her last moment on this earth, is special to God. Pope John Paul was an apostle of life who warned against fostering a culture of death. He himself had lived through very difficult times. He had seen the persecution and invasion of his own country. He had experienced the horrors of war. He had witnessed what seemed to be total disregard of his people and culture. All of this only strengthened John Paul's firm belief in the dignity and worth of every human being.

The pope's second letter, *Rich in Mercy*, calls everyone's attention to our Savior as the God of mercy. "I want people to be convinced of how much our Savior loves us," Pope John Paul said. "No one need ever be afraid of God. And if God loves us, we need not fear anyone or anything. We never have to be afraid."

"Do not be afraid," was a message John Paul never tired of repeating. He lived these words until the last moment of his life. John Paul knew that fear keeps us apart from God and prevents us from loving God. And we should never let that happen.

The pope also called the bishops to Rome and led Church meetings called synods (*sin-odds*). When possible, he spoke in the language of the person or audience that he addressed. The Polish Pope spoke eight languages fluently. *Time* magazine named him Man of the Year in 1994. Pope John Paul II was making history.

So many other wonderful accomplishments are all part of John Paul's life and legacy. But the greatest lessons he would "preach" without saying a word were still to come . . .

20

THE FATHER'S HOUSE

The Holy Father had always been an admirer of the saints and blesseds of the Catholic Church. So many people, he believed, could be inspired in the daily living of their own lives by the example of these holy persons.

Over the years, the pope proclaimed 1,338 persons blessed (the step before sainthood) and canonized 482 saints—the greatest number of any pope in history. These holy witnesses were from all over the world, spoke a wide variety of languages, and came from different cultures. They each had a particular lesson to offer. The pope realized that people could pray to God through the intercession of these holy men, women, and children to seek the help and guidance they needed.

Pope John Paul also declared the Great Jubilee of the Year 2000. That was a celebration of the 2,000th anniversary of the birth of Jesus. Previously, in 1988, the pope had proclaimed a Marian Year in honor of the Blessed Mother.

Pope John Paul II began World Youth Day, a gathering of young people held every two years in a different country. He also initiated the World Day of the Sick, celebrated every year on February 11, the feast of Our Lady of Lourdes.

As the years passed, John Paul's physical health began to fail, but not his enthusiasm and zest for life. During the 1990s, he suffered from a benign tumor, an injured shoulder, a broken thighbone, and various infections. He also developed a disease of the nervous system called Parkinson's disease. Breathing and eventually even speaking became difficult and painful. The beloved pope grew more and more frail.

On Easter Sunday in 2005, Pope John Paul sat at his apartment window to greet the crowds in Saint Peter's Square. The words formed slowly on his lips, but no sound came out. Instead, he made the sign of the cross several times.

The pope was very ill. He chose to stay in his Vatican bedroom rather than return to Gemelli Hospital. He knew the end was near, and he wanted to die at home.

During those last weeks of illness, John Paul reflected gratefully that his own native land had, at last, been freed from the tyranny of Communism. He thanked the Lord for the elections held in Poland in 1989 and for the fall of the Berlin Wall that same year. He thought back on the many blessings and graces with which the Lord had filled his life and, through him, the lives of so many others.

When it became clear that the Holy Father was dying, Father Stanislaw, other close friends, and the Vatican household gathered around him. They prayed for him and with him, and John Paul received the Anointing of the Sick. Outside, in Saint Peter's Square, a crowd of 70,000—many of them young people—waited and prayed. John Paul had always been there for them. Now, in gratitude, they had come to offer him their love and the support of their prayers.

"I want to go home now, to my heavenly Father," the eighty-four-year-old pope finally whispered in Polish. He glanced at the framed photo of his parents on their wedding day. He looked gratefully at Father Stanislaw, his trusted friend for so many years. Soon his eyes looked straight ahead. They were no longer seeing the things of this world. They were beholding the face of God.

Pope John Paul II went home to our heavenly Father at 9:37 PM on Saturday, April 2,

2005. It was the vigil of Divine Mercy Sunday—a feast that John Paul himself had given to the Church in response to the request Jesus had made of the Polish nun Saint Faustina Kowalska.

Nearly four million people from all over the world traveled to Rome for the funeral of John Paul II. They included heads of state from 138 countries. At his funeral, many people cried out, "*Santo Subito!*—Make him a saint soon!"

On June 28, 2005, the opening of the cause of Pope John Paul II's beatification was held at the Basilica of Saint John Lateran in Rome. Although it often takes many years before a person is declared "blessed," so many people admired John Paul II as a follower of Jesus that he was beatified only six years after his death. He was declared "blessed" on May, 1, 2011, Divine Mercy Sunday.

Only three years later, on April 27, 2014, John Paul II was canonized by Pope Francis.

Pope John Paul II was a courageous and loving leader of the Church. He reached out to young and old alike, traveling around the world to help everyone know the love of Jesus and to be courageous in following him. His life continues to inspire people everywhere—for, truly, he was the people's pope.

PRAYER

Saint John Paul II, you are one of the great gifts of our Church and of our century. You lived your life to the full with courage and enthusiasm. Thank you for showing us how to follow Jesus during challenging times. You never let oppression and tyranny spoil your dreams nor dampen your faith.

Because of the media and modern means of travel, you became the most well-known pope in history. You came into our families through television, radio, and the Internet. Your message came into our hearts because of who you were—a man of peace and hope. You reminded us over and over: Do not be afraid.

Sometimes, even though I don't want to be, I am afraid. I ask you to help me to live in strong faith and unselfish love. Please ask Jesus to give me the strength I need to be and to remain his true follower. Pray that, like you, Saint John Paul, I will always keep close to the Blessed Mother, who leads us all to Jesus. Amen.

GLOSSARY

1. Anointing of the Sick—the sacrament in which the Holy Spirit strengthens and gives courage and peace to someone who is seriously ill. God's Spirit, through this sacrament, forgives sin and heals the soul.

2. Assassin—a person who tries to kill a well-known leader or world figure.

3. Beatification—the ceremony in which the Catholic Church recognizes that a deceased person lived a life of Gospel holiness in a heroic way. In most cases, a proven miracle obtained through the holy person's prayers to God is also required. A person who is beatified is given the title Blessed.

4. Candlemas Day—a feast day, celebrated on February 2, in honor of the purification of Mary and the presentation of Jesus in the Temple. It is now referred to as the feast of the Presentation of the Lord. Traditionally, candles are blessed on this day, and candlelight processions are often held.

5. Canonization—the ceremony in which the pope officially declares that someone is a saint in heaven. To canonize someone is to recognize that he or she has lived a life of heroic virtue, is worthy of imitation, and can intercede for others. Like beatification, which it follows, canonization requires a miracle resulting from the holy person's prayers to God.

6. Capuchin—a branch of the Franciscan order. Capuchin friars live lives of poverty and simplicity. The Capuchins have gained wide respect as preachers, missionaries, and confessors.

7. Cassock—A long, close-fitting garment, sometimes belted, that is worn by priests. For everyday wear, cassocks are generally black, although bishops may wear purple cassocks and cardinals may wear red. The cassock of the pope is always white.

8. Communism—A repressive political system in which the government controls the economy and a single party holds power. In theory, all property and production would be owned in common, rather than by individuals. Communism was the economic and political system of the Soviet Union and its satellite nations for much of the twentieth century. Pope John Paul II is widely considered one of the world leaders whose influence brought about the end of Soviet Communism.

9. Conclave—the private meetings at the Vatican in which the cardinals elect a new pope. During the conclave, no outsiders are permitted to communicate with the cardinals.

10. Concentration camp—a guarded prison compound where Jews, members of ethnic minorities, and political opponents of the Nazis were confined, mistreated, and often killed prior to and during World War II.

11. Encyclical letter—a papal document that explores and explains matters related to the teachings of the Church. Encyclicals are sent from the pope to the bishops and the people of the Church. They express the pope's thoughts on faith, morality, and other religious topics.

12. Gestapo—the German state secret police during the years of the Nazi regime. The Gestapo was first organized in 1933 and was much feared for its brutality.

13. Gregorian chant—a form of musical worship named after Pope Gregory I (590–

604). Gregorian chant may have originally begun with Jewish sources. It is the oldest form of religious chant used today.

14. Lay person—a non-clergy member of the church.

15. Mentor—a wise and trusted counselor or teacher.

16. Nazi Party—the National Socialist German Workers' party, which, under Adolf Hitler, seized political control of Germany in 1933. The Nazis suppressed all those who opposed them. They were responsible for the imprisonment and murder of more than 6 million Jews as well as millions of other people. The party was officially abolished in 1945 at the end of World War II.

17. Niche—an ornamental opening in a wall, usually semicircular and arched, that displays a statue or other decorative object.

18. Parkinson's disease—a disorder of the central nervous system. Patients may experience rigid muscles, trembling, and slowing or loss of movement. Walking can become difficult, and speech may also be affected. There is no cure for Parkinson's disease, but medications can provide relief in some cases.

19. Prelate—a priest of a high order, as a bishop, archbishop, or cardinal; a church dignitary.

20. Seminary—a special school providing academic and religious education to prepare students for the priesthood.

21. Thesis—a long essay on a specialized subject for which the writer has done original research. Often a thesis is a requirement for a graduate degree. Some theses are published as books.

22. Transfiguration, feast of—a feast day commemorating the wonderful event of Jesus letting Peter, James, and John witness his divine glory. It is celebrated on August 6.

23. The Vatican—the central authority and government of the Catholic Church. The buildings of the Vatican Palace, near the Basilica of Saint Peter in Vatican City, include the main residence of the pope. Only a small part of the palace is used as living quarters; the rest consists of offices and museums. Vatican City, an independent state, lies within the boundaries of Rome, Italy, and covers 108.7 acres.

Who are the Daughters of St. Paul?

We are Catholic sisters. Our mission is to be like Saint Paul and tell everyone about Jesus! There are so many ways for people to communicate with each other. We want to use all of them so everyone will know how much God loves them. We do this by printing books (you're holding one!), making radio shows, singing, helping people at our bookstores, using the Internet, and in many other ways.

Visit our website at www.pauline.org

Pauline
BOOKS & MEDIA

The Daughters of St. Paul operate book and media centers at the following addresses. Visit, call or write the one nearest you today, or find us at www.paulinestore.org.

CALIFORNIA
3908 Sepulveda Blvd, Culver City, CA 90230   310-397-8676
3250 Middlefield Road, Menlo Park, CA 94025   650-369-4230

FLORIDA
145 S.W. 107th Avenue, Miami, FL 33174   305-559-6715

HAWAII
1143 Bishop Street, Honolulu, HI 96813   808-521-2731

ILLINOIS
172 North Michigan Avenue, Chicago, IL 60601   312-346-4228

LOUISIANA
4403 Veterans Memorial Blvd, Metairie, LA 70006   504-887-7631

MASSACHUSETTS
885 Providence Hwy, Dedham, MA 02026   781-326-5385

MISSOURI
9804 Watson Road, St. Louis, MO 63126   314-965-3512

NEW YORK
115 E. 29th Street, New York City, NY 10016   212-754-1110

SOUTH CAROLINA
243 King Street, Charleston, SC 29401   843-577-0175

TEXAS
No book center; for parish exhibits or outreach evangelization, contact: 210-569-0500, or SanAntonio@paulinemedia.com, or P.O. Box 761416, San Antonio, TX 78245

VIRGINIA
1025 King Street, Alexandria, VA 22314   703-549-3806

CANADA
3022 Dufferin Street, Toronto, ON M6B 3T5   416-781-9131

¡También somos su fuente
para libros, videos y música en español!